# 2 Regular Guys Cookbook

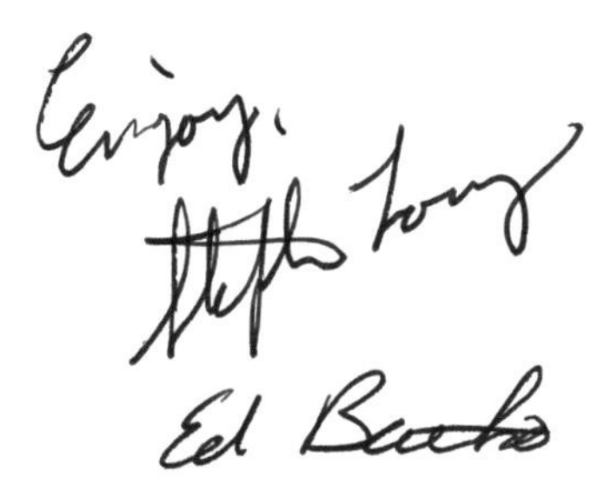

# 2 REGULAR GUYS COOKBOOK

## Menus and Other Tidbits for the Football Season

**Ed Bartko & Steve Long**

THE SUMMIT PUBLISHING GROUP

IRVING, TEXAS

THE SUMMIT PUBLISHING GROUP



*Printed in the United States of America*
05 04 03 02 01 00 6 5 4 3 2 1

**Library of Congress Cataloging-in-Publication Data**
Barkto, Ed, 1961–
2 regular guys cookbook : menus and other tidbits for the footbal season / Ed Bartko & Steve Long.
p. cm.
ISBN 1–56530-308-3
1. Snack foods. 2. Menus. 4. Footbal players. I. Title: Two regular guys cookbook. II. Long, Steve, 1961– III. Title.
TX740.B385 2000
641.8'12—dc21 00–058367

# About the Book

The idea of a regular sports fan cookbook came about when my neighbor and I started getting together to watch football each week. One week we would meet at my house and then the next week at his house. We started off at my house, and I had some chips, dip, and sodas on hand for the game. The next week my neighbor had chips, dip, sodas, and chicken wings. Well, the week after that I had chips, dip, sodas, chicken wings, and sausage balls. Before the end of the season we were cooking enough food to feed an army of sports fans just trying to outdo each other. We had a lot of fun and realized that others might enjoy some of the easy recipes that we compiled and created in our own Regular Guys way.

In this book you will find easy-to-make food that will make any sporting event more enjoyable. We have included seventeen complete menus, a Super Bowl Sunday Spectacular, a list of recipes so you can mix and match if you choose, and trivia questions to make your sporting event the best of times. There are even a few extra goodies. The recipes for each week fall into three groups:

- First Half Appetizers (appetizers)
- The Half-Time Show (entrees)
- The Last Half (dessert)

Our recipes can serve up to eight people comfortably. Answers to the trivia questions can be found on page 101.

Out of the cookbook came the idea that there were other things regular guys would like to know about from the perspective of other regular guys. As we sat and talked about things during the game we realized that a regular guys opinion is never heard. We always have had sports analysts or government analysts or our wives tell us how we are supposed to think. Well, we thought it was time to think and speak for ourselves. So out of this we created a website, **www.tworegularguys.com**, which is dedicated to all the regular guys who want to finally be heard. On this site regular guys can respond, speak up, and tell us what's on their mind. So log on and tell us what you like to eat, tell us what you like to do and how to do it.

# Week 1

1. Who has the highest winning percentage of any professional football coach in his first 100 wins?

# Menu #1

**Creamy Salsa Dip and Tortilla Chips**
**Ranch Buffalo Wings**
**Eclair Pie**

## Creamy Salsa Dip

2 (8 ounce) packages cream cheese
2 cups salsa

Soften cream cheese until smooth, add salsa, mix well and refrigerate. Serve with tortilla chips.

## Ranch Buffalo Wings

½ cup butter, melted
¼ cup hot sauce
3 tablespoons vinegar
24 chicken wings
1 package ranch salad dressing mix

Preheat oven to 350 degrees. In a small bowl, whisk together butter, hot sauce, and vinegar. Dip wings into the mixture.

Arrange in a single layer in a large baking pan. Sprinkle on dry salad dressing mix. Bake for 40 minutes or until chicken is brown and juices run clear when pierced.

## Eclair Pie

1 box graham crackers
2 small boxes instant vanilla pudding, prepared
1 (12 ounce) container whipped topping
1 can of chocolate frosting

Line the bottom of a 9 x 13 baking pan with graham crackers. Mix pudding according to directions on the box. Add thawed whipped topping to the pudding mixture. Spoon mixture into pan. Break remaining graham crackers into squares and frost with chocolate frosting. Place frosted squares on top of pudding mixture. Chill in the refrigerator for two hours.

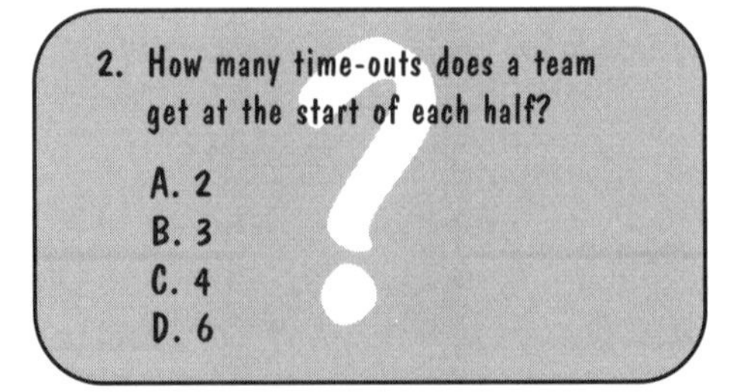

## PLAYER PROFILE

**Joe Montana** was drafted by the San Francisco 49ers in 1979 from the University of Notre Dame. While with the 49ers Joe led the team to 4 Super Bowl titles, and was named the Most Valuable Player in 3 of those games. Montana left the 49ers and ended his career as a Kansas City Chief. He is a sure bet to be inducted into the Professional Football Hall of Fame. Montana, however, is not out of competitive sports. He has moved from the football field to the field of auto racing. Joe is a member of the Target/Chip Ganassi Racing Team. The Ganassi team is a major dominator on the CART circuit. He loves racing and intends to be a part of the racing circuit for a long time.

# Week 2

3. What two professional football teams played the first regular season overtime game which ended in a tie after the overtime period?

# Menu #2

## Deviled Eggs

## Smokies

## Chocolate Chip Cheesecake

### Deviled Eggs

1 dozen eggs
Mayonnaise (to taste)
Relish (to taste)
1 cup celery, chopped

Boil eggs for 10 minutes. Cool and peel. Slice eggs lengthwise. Scoop out yolk and mix with mayonnaise, relish, and celery. Fill sliced eggs and chill to serve.

### Smokies

1 package small Smokies sausages
1 bottle barbeque sauce

Combine sausages, barbeque sauce in a crock pot, and cook on low heat for a minimum of 3 hours.

## Chocolate Chip Cheesecake

6 ounces cream cheese, softened
1 (14 ounce) can sweetened condensed milk
1 egg
1 teaspoon vanilla extract
½ cup mini chocolate chips
1 teaspoon flour
1 (6 ounce) ready-made chocolate pie crust
1 jar chocolate sauce

Preheat oven to 350 degrees. Using a mixer beat cheese until fluffy. Gradually beat in condensed milk until smooth. Add egg and vanilla and mix well. Toss chips with flour and then stir them into the cheese mixture. Pour mixture into crust. Bake for 35 minutes. Let cheesecake stand and cool, then top with chocolate sauce.

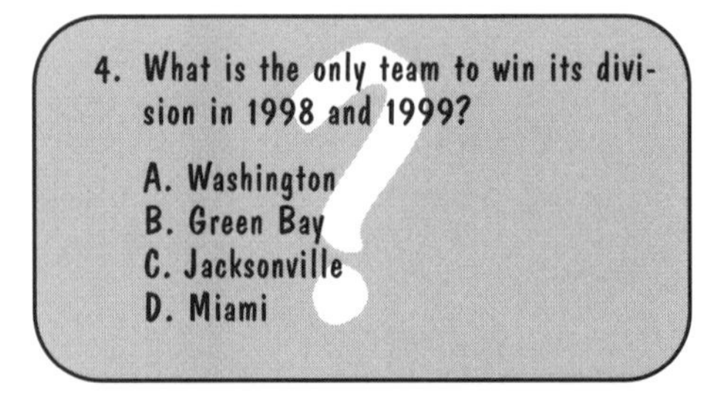

# Week 3

5. After the merger of the AFL and the NFL what was the first NFL team to lose to an AFL team?

# Menu #3

Hot Crab Dip

Chicken Quesadillas

Cream Cookie Dessert

## Hot Crab Dip

- 16 ounces cream cheese, softened
- 12 ounces crabmeat
- ½ cup shredded Parmesan cheese
- ¼ cup chopped green onions
- 2 tablespoons white wine
- 2 teaspoons horseradish
- ¼ teaspoon hot pepper sauce

Mix all ingredients with a mixer on medium speed until well blended. Spoon into 9-inch pie plate. Bake at 350 degrees for 30 minutes.

## Chicken Quesadillas

- 1 pound boneless chicken breast, cubed
- 1 can Cheddar cheese soup

½ cup salsa
16 ounces sour cream
1 bunch green onions, finely chopped
10 flour tortillas

Preheat oven to 450 degrees. In a nonstick pan cook chicken for 5 minutes over medium to high heat or until done. Add soup and salsa and heat through. Place tortillas on baking sheets. Fill each tortilla with ⅓ cup of mixture, roll up and bake for 5 minutes. Top with sour cream and onions.

## Cream Cookie Dessert

24 crushed chocolate sandwich cookies
½ stick melted butter
½ gallon vanilla ice cream packaged in a square container
1 cup chocolate syrup
1 (8 ounce) container whipped topping
1 small can salted peanuts

Mix and press crushed cookies and butter into a 9 x 13 pan. Slice ice cream and lay on top of crust. Freeze for ½ hour. Drizzle syrup over ice cream and freeze for ½ hour. Spread whipped topping and nuts on top and freeze until ready to serve.

## PLAYER PROFILE

**Roger Staubach** was drafted by the Dallas Cowboys in 1964 from the Naval Academy. Staubach was a Heisman Trophy winner in college but while with the Cowboys, he led them to 4 Super Bowl appearances and 2 titles. He was elected to the Professional Football Hall of Fame in 1985. Staubach is still earning high honors, but now it is in the field of business. He is a sought-after speaker on the sales lecture circuit. Roger is also the CEO of the Staubach Company, which is a blue-chip real estate and corporate relocation firm based in Dallas.

# Week 4

6. What player has the most years of service playing football?

# Menu #4

**Bean Dip**

**Beef Kabobs**

**Dirt Pudding**

## Bean Dip

1 (4 ounce) can chopped ripe olives
½ cup minced onion
¼ cup taco sauce
1 teaspoon garlic salt
1 (29 ounce) can refried beans
1 ¼ cup shredded Cheddar cheese

Preheat oven to 350 degrees. Combine refried beans, olives, onion, taco sauce, garlic salt, and 1 cup of cheese. Spoon into a 1-quart baking dish, top with remaining cheese and bake for 30 minutes. Serve with tortilla chips.

## Beef Kabobs

2 pounds beef tips
1 bottle meat marinade
1 large green pepper, cut into large pieces
1 large red pepper, cut into large pieces
1 large onion and tomato, cut into large chunks

Marinate beef tips in refrigerator overnight. Preheat grill to medium heat. Place a beef tip, green pepper, red pepper, onion, and tomato onto skewer. Repeat till skewer is full. Wrap kabob in foil and place on grill for 15 minutes. Check meat to see if done. Rewrap and place back on grill till done to personal satisfaction.

## Dirt Pudding

1 large package chocolate sandwich cookies
1 stick margarine melted
2 boxes instant vanilla pudding, prepared
8 ounces cream cheese
1 cup powdered sugar
1 (12 ounce) container whipped cream

Crush up cookies and set aside 1 cup for later use. Mix together the rest of the cookies with the margarine. Press the mixture into a 9 x 13 pan. Mix the two boxes of pudding together according to the directions on the box. Set aside. Mix together 8 ounces of cream cheese and 1 cup of powdered sugar and add to the pudding mix. Fold in the whipped cream with the pudding mixture and then pour on top of the crushed cookies. Top the pudding with the 1 cup of set aside cookies and chill for 2 hours.

# Week 5

7. Who holds the record for consecutive games scoring a touchdown?

# Menu #5

Dijon Bacon Dip

Sausage Balls

Quick Banana Pie

## Dijon Bacon Dip

1 cup mayonnaise
½ cup Dijon mustard
4 strips bacon, cooked and crumbled
1 tablespoon horseradish

Mix all ingredients together and chill till serving time.

## Sausage Balls

1 pound ground pork sausage
8 ounces shredded Cheddar cheese
1 cup of Bisquick

Preheat oven to 350 degrees. Mix all ingredients well. Form mixture into small balls. Bake for 20 minutes on a baking pan, not a cookie sheet.

## Quick Banana Pie

1 baked pie shell
1 large box vanilla instant pudding, prepared
8 ounces sour cream
2 or more bananas
1 (8 ounce) container of whipped topping

Prepare pudding according to directions on box. Stir in the sour cream. Slice bananas into the pie shell, then pour the filling over them. Top with whipped topping and refrigerate till time to serve.

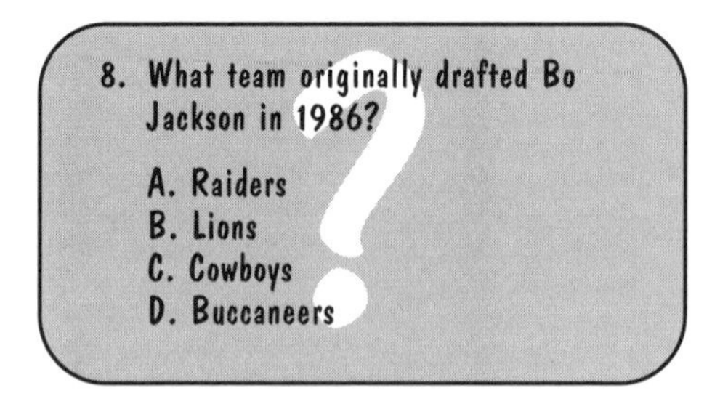

## PLAYER PROFILE

**Walter Payton,** aka Sweetness, was drafted by the Chicago Bears in 1975 from Jackson State in Mississippi. He was a 2-time NFL Most Valuable Player and won 1 Super Bowl title with the Bears. Payton was inducted into the Professional Football Hall of Fame in 1993 and still holds the all-time rushing record. Walter had another love in life. In addition to a multitude of business pursuits, "Sweetness" was committed to the neediest children in Illinois through the Walter Payton Foundation and the Alliance for the Children. In spite of his fatal rare liver disease, he worked tirelessly to provide Christmas gifts, promote adoptions, scholarships and employment opportunities for wards of the state. Walter Payton died in November 1999.

# Week 6

9. Who kicked the most field goals over 50 yards in one game?

# Menu #6

**Vegetable Dip**

**Chili**

**Cheesecake Squares**

## Vegetable Dip

2 teaspoons garlic powder
½ cup sugar
3 tablespoons oil
2 teaspoons prepared mustard
1 cup mayonnaise

Mix all ingredients, except mayonnaise, and let stand 1 hour. Add 1 cup of mayonnaise and serve with your choice of raw or parboiled vegetables.

## Chili

2 pounds ground sirloin
1 cup chopped onions
1 green pepper, chopped
1 clove garlic
1 ½ tablespoons chili powder

2 jalapeño peppers
½ teaspoon cumin
½ teaspoon oregano
½ teaspoon salt
2 ½ cups water
2 tablespoons vegetable oil
1 (15 ounce) can chili beans

In a large pan heat oil and brown the ground sirloin. Add onions, green pepper, and garlic. Cook for 10 minutes. Add all remaining ingredients and simmer for 2 hours.

## Cheesecake Squares

1 package chocolate sandwich cookies, divided
2 tablespoons butter, melted
32 ounces cream cheese, softened
1 cup of sugar
1 teaspoon of vanilla
4 beaten eggs

Preheat oven to 350 degrees. Ground twenty cookies into a powder, add butter and mix well. Press mixture into the bottom of a 9 x 13 inch baking pan. Chop up an additional 15 cookies and set aside. Mix cream cheese, sugar, and vanilla with a mixer until well blended. Add eggs and mix until blended. Stir in the 15 chopped-up cookies and pour into pan. Bake for 40 minutes. Refrigerate overnight.

# Week 7

10. Who holds the record for most consecutive seasons with 1,000 yards rushing?

# Menu #7

### Macaroni Salad

### Super Sub

### Better-Than-Golf Cake

## Macaroni Salad

2 cups uncooked macaroni
2 green peppers
1 red pepper
1 golden pepper
2 stalks celery
1 small onion
1 (16 once) jar salad dressing
Seasoning salt to taste

Cook macaroni and drain according to directions on package. Chop vegetables up into bite-size pieces, rinse and drain. Combine macaroni, vegetables and salad dressing (we like Miracle Whip). Season to taste—usually about 3 to 4 tablespoons. Chill until ready to serve.

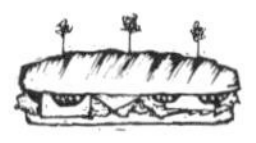

## Super Sub

¼ pound turkey breast
⅓ pound swiss cheese
¼ pound roast beef
⅓ pound Colby-Jack cheese
¼ pound ham
1 head lettuce, shredded
2 ripe tomatoes, thinly sliced
12 ounces of your favorite sandwich dressing
1 loaf French bread, sliced lengthwise

Starting on the bottom half of the bread layer as follows: turkey, swiss cheese, roast beef, Colby-Jack cheese, ham, lettuce, tomatoes. Spread your favorite dressing on the top half of the bread and cover the sandwich. Cut into desired lengths and enjoy.

**11. What player holds the record for most receiving yards in one game?**

**A. Herman Moore**
**B. Flipper Anderson**
**C. Randy Moss**
**D. Jerry Rice**

## Better-Than-Golf Cake

1 package German chocolate cake mix
1 can sweetened condensed milk
1 jar butterscotch-caramel sauce
1 container whipped topping
1 bag toffee chips

Prepare cake following directions on the package. As soon as cake is taken from the oven, poke holes in the top with a fork. The more holes the better. Pour condensed milk over the entire cake. Then pour the butterscotch-caramel sauce over the cake. Put into freezer for 45 minutes. Top with whipped topping and toffee chips.

**12. Who was the most recent starting AFC quarterback to win a Super Bowl other than John Elway?**

**A. Boomer Esiason**
**B. Bernie Kosar**
**C. Dan Marino**
**D. Jim Plunkett**

## PLAYER PROFILE

**Eric Dickerson** was the second overall pick by the Rams in 1983 from SMU. Dickerson was voted rookie of the year in his first season with a record 1,808 yards of rushing and a record 18 touchdowns. He went on to have a great career, reaching the 10,000-yard mark in 91 games, quicker than anyone else in NFL history. Eric is a Hall of Famer who now lives in Malibu, California. In retirment, he spends a great deal of time supporting and promoting various charities such as 2nd Byte, a program that helps at-risk students, the Muscular Dystrophy Association, and Courage 4 Life, an organization that helps those in need of extreme medical treatment like bone marrow transplant.

# Week 8

13. Who had the highest pass rating as a rookie quarterback?

# Menu #8

Tortilla Cheese Dip

Bratwurst

Cool Lemonade Pie

## Tortilla Cheese Dip

4 jalapeño peppers, chopped up
2 cans Cheddar cheese soup
2 cans condensed milk
2 pounds processed cheese, cubed

Combine ingredients in sauce pan and heat on medium low till all cheese is melted. Serve with tortilla chips.

## Bratwurst

2 pounds bratwurst
¼ cup vegetable oil
3 green peppers, cut into ¼-inch strips
1 large sweet onion, cut into ¼-inch slices
4 hoagie rolls

Preheat grill to a medium high temperature. Pour oil into a disposable aluminum pan. Put sausage, peppers, and onions into pan and cover with foil. Place pan onto the center of the grill. Cook for 20 minutes, stirring the contents three or four times. After 20 minutes remove bratwurst and cook on grill for an additional 6 minutes to brown. Serve on hoagie rolls with favorite toppings. For added taste, toast rolls on the grill for a few moments.

## Cool Lemonade Pie

1 (6 ounce) can frozen lemonade
1 (14 ounce) can sweetened condensed milk
1 (9 inch) graham cracker crust
1 (8 ounce) container whipped topping

Mix lemonade and condensed milk thoroughly, pour into pie crust, and top with whipped topping. Refrigerate for a minimum of 4 hours.

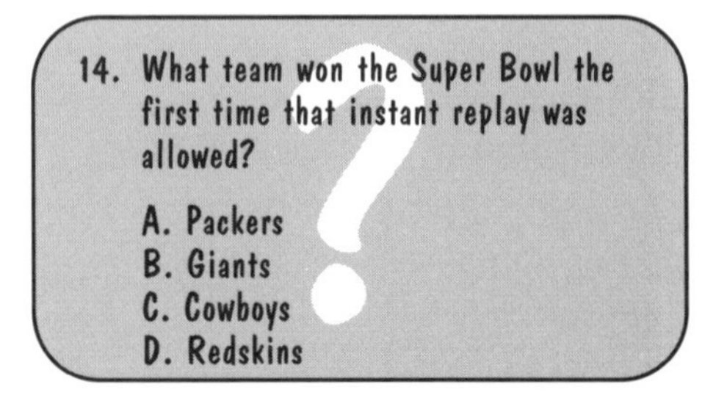

14. What team won the Super Bowl the first time that instant replay was allowed?

A. Packers
B. Giants
C. Cowboys
D. Redskins

# Week 9

15. Who holds the highest completion percentage during a Super Bowl with at least 20 attempts?

### Fourth-And-Long Chicken Tortillas

### Texas Blow-Out

### Sensational Brownies

## Fourth-And-Long Chicken Tortillas

1 jar salsa
¼ cup sour cream
1 pound boneless, skinless chicken breast, cooked and shredded
1 bag tortilla chips
1 cup shredded Cheddar cheese

Combine salsa, sour cream, and chicken in a bowl. Spread chips out on a baking sheet. Spread chicken mixture over chips. Top with cheese and bake at 400 degrees till cheese melts. Serve immediately.

## Texas Blow-Out

1 pound hamburger, browned and drained
½ pound bacon, fried and drained
1 onion, chopped

½ cup ketchup
¾ cups brown sugar
1 tablespoon vinegar
1 tablespoon dry mustard
1 can pork and beans
1 can lima beans, drained
1 can kidney beans, drained

Preheat oven to 350 degrees. Mix all ingredients and bake for 1 hour. Serve in bowls with bread of your choice.

## Sensational Brownies

1 ½ cup butter, melted
3 cups sugar
1 tablespoon vanilla
5 eggs
1 cup cocoa
2 cups flour
1 teaspoon baking powder
1 teaspoon salt

Preheat oven to 350 degrees. Grease a 9 x 13 inch pan. In a bowl stir together the butter, sugar, and vanilla. Add eggs and stir until well blended. Stir in cocoa, flour, baking powder, and salt. Blend well. Spread batter in prepared pan. Bake for 55 minutes. Cool and cut into squares.

## PLAYER PROFILE

**Ozzie Newsome** was a first-round draft pick by the Browns in 1978. Newsome was nicknamed the Wizard of Oz for his improbable catches. The Oz went on to have a Hall-of-Fame career, retiring with a record 662 receptions for tight ends. Newsome is the fourth-leading receiver overall. He built his stellar career in Cleveland but now is building a new legacy as Vice President of Player Personnel for the Baltimore Ravens.

# Week 10

16. Which two NFC teams have no retired uniform numbers?

# Menu #10

Beef Cheese Ball

Sloppy Joes

Surprise Pie

## Beef Cheese Ball

2 (8 ounce) packages cream cheese, softened
1 green pepper, chopped finely
1 (2 ounce) jar dried beef, chopped into small pieces
⅓ cup Italian dressing
1 cup walnuts, coarsely chopped (optional)

Mix all ingredients well. Shape into ball, and roll in nuts if desired. Chill. Let stand at room temperature 30 minutes before serving.

## Sloppy Joes

1 pound ground beef
½ onion, finely chopped
½ cup ketchup
2 tablespoons brown sugar

2 tablespoons vinegar
1 tablespoon Worcestershire sauce
2 tablespoons prepared mustard

Brown and drain the ground beef. Add remaining ingredients. Simmer for 15 minutes.

## Surprise Pie

1 (9 inch) prepared graham cracker pie crust
2 large chocolate almond bars
18 ounces whipped topping

Melt chocolate almond bars. Cool to room temperature. Mix together with whipped topping. Pour into pie crust and refrigerate.

17. What Raider defensive back knocked the ball loose on the famous "Immaculate Reception" play during the Raiders/Steelers game of the 70's?

A. Lester Hayes
B. Jack Ham
C. Cliff Harris
D. Jack Tatum

# Week 11

18. What team has the most game victories and defeats in a Super Bowl?

# Menu #11

Mexican Rollups

Sausage Vegetable Soup

Moon Cake

## Mexican Rollups

16 ounces sour cream
16 ounces cream cheese, softened
1 bunch green onions, chopped
3 jalapeño peppers, chopped
1 jar picante sauce
1 package soft tortillas

Mix all ingredients together well. Spread onto tortillas and roll up. Place on a cookie sheet and refrigerate overnight. Slice into 1-inch pieces.

## Sausage Vegetable Soup

1 pound mixed dried beans
1 (28 ounce) can whole tomatoes, chopped
1 red pepper, chopped
1 green pepper, chopped

2 ½ cups peas, whole kernel corn, green beans
3 carrots, chopped
3 stalks celery, chopped
1 onion, chopped
1 (14 ounce) can chicken broth
2 pounds sausage links

Rinse beans thoroughly, place in a large pot, and cover with water. Bring to a boil for 5 minutes. Cover and let stand in refrigerator overnight. Drain and rinse beans. Combine beans with tomatoes, vegetables, and broth. Cover and cook on low for 8 hours, adding water if needed. Saute sausage until done and cut into ¼-inch pieces. Add meat to soup and cook another 40 minutes.

## Moon Cake

1 (9 inch) prepared pie crust
1 large box vanilla pudding
1 package cream cheese
1 (8 ounce) container whipped topping
1 jar chocolate sauce
1 package chopped nuts

Mix pudding according to package directions. Add cream cheese. Blend well and pour into crust. Refrigerate for 20 minutes and top with whipped topping, chocolate sauce, and nuts.

## PLAYER PROFILE

**Steve Largent** was a record-setting pass receiver for the Seahawks from 1976-1989. Largent was acquired by the Seahawks in a preseason trade with Houston. Steve led the NFL in receiving in 1979 and 1985. After his retirement from football, Largent continued to lead but in a different arena: the arena of politics. Today he is a congressman from Oklahoma. He was chosen to fill the unexpired term of James Inhofe and was later re-elected for full terms in 1996 and 1998.

# Week 12

19. What team scored the most points in a Super Bowl and against what team?

# Menu #12

Dill Dip

BBQ Meatballs

Key Lime Pie

## Dill Dip

1 teaspoon seasoned salt
1 tablespoon dried dill
1 cup sour cream
½ cup mayonnaise

Mix all ingredients, cover and chill for 3 hours. Serve with veggies or chips.

## B-B-Q Meatballs

*Meatballs*
½ pound ground sirloin
½ pound ground turkey
½ cup bread crumbs
½ teaspoon garlic salt

¼ teaspoon pepper
1/8 cup ketchup

*Sauce*
½ bottle barbeque sauce
1 small can tomato sauce
2 tablespoons flour
½ cup water

Mix all of the meatball ingredients together and form into small balls. Bake in baking dish for 30 minutes at 250 degrees. Drain off any grease. Stir together all sauce ingredients and pour sauce over meatballs and bake for an additional 20 minutes.

## Key Lime Pie

1 (9 inch) graham cracker crust
1 (14 ounce) can sweetened condensed milk
2 egg yolks
½ cup lime juice
1 (8 ounce) container whipped topping

Beat condensed milk, egg yolks, and lime juice until thick. Pour into pie shell and chill overnight. Cover with whipped topping and serve immediately.

# Week 13

20. What is the longest fumble recovery returned for a touchdown?

# Menu #13

Steve's Spinach Dip

Ed's Chimichanga

Chocolate Cream Pie

## Steve's Spinach Dip

1 package (10 ounce) frozen spinach
1 envelope vegetable soup mix
½ cup mayonnaise
1 ½ cup sour cream
1 teaspoon lemon juice

Thaw spinach and drain. Mix all ingredients well and chill 4 hours before serving. Serve with veggies or crackers.

## Ed's Chimichanga

1 pound hamburger, cooked and drained
1 package taco seasoning
1 (16 ounce) can refried beans
8 tortillas (your choice, corn or flour)
1 head shredded lettuce

12 ounces shredded Cheddar cheese
Chopped tomatoes and onions

In skillet combine hamburger, taco seasoning, and refried beans. Put ¼ cup filling into tortilla. Fold center to center, overlapping slightly. Fold up ends and secure with a toothpick. Fry in skillet until golden brown. Serve with lettuce, cheese, tomatoes, and onions.

## Chocolate Cream Pie

1 (9 inch) graham cracker pie crust
2 (4 ounce) boxes chocolate pudding, prepared
1 (16 ounce) container whipped topping

Prepare pudding according to instructions on package. Mix in whipped topping and pour into pie shell. Chill 4 hours before serving.

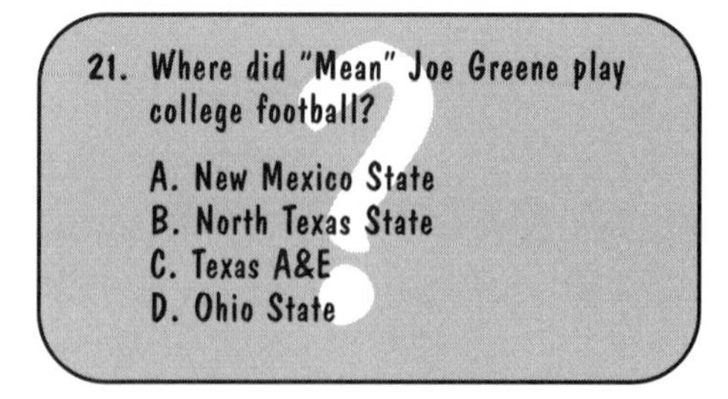

21. Where did "Mean" Joe Greene play college football?

A. New Mexico State
B. North Texas State
C. Texas A&E
D. Ohio State

## PLAYER PROFILE

**Anthony Munoz** was the Bengals' 3rd overall selection in the 1980 draft, then went on to be an all-pro for 11 straight years, had 11 consecutive selections to the Pro Bowl, and was defensive lineman of the year in 1981, 85, 88, and 89. Munoz started 177 games of 178. He is the first full-time player of the Bengals to be inducted into the Hall of Fame. But did you know that he almost did not get a chance to play in the NFL. Munoz had 3 knee operations in college and failed physical examinations by 14 NFL teams. The Bengals took a chance and are glad they did.

# Week 14

22. Where did Dallas Cowboy's star quarterback, Roger Staubach, play college football?

# Menu #14

## Hamburger Cheese Dip
## Chicken BBQ Delight
## Chocolate Chip Cookies

### Hamburger Cheese Dip

1 pound lean ground beef
1 pound processed cheese
1 can tomatoes with green chilles
1 teaspoon chili powder

Brown and drain ground beef. Melt cheese and mix with remaining ingredients. Add beef. Serve with corn chips of your choice

### Chicken B-B-Q Delight

21 ounce bottle barbeque sauce
1 package dry onion soup mix
2 pounds chicken

Preheat oven to 350 degrees. Pour half of BBQ sauce and soup mix into bottom of a 9 x 13 inch pan. Lay chicken pieces in, pour rest of barbeque sauce over chicken, and sprinkle with remaining soup mix. Bake for 1 hour.

## Chocolate Chip Cookies

2 ¼ cup flour
1 teaspoon baking soda
1 teaspoon salt
1 cup butter flavor shortening
¾ cup sugar
¾ cup packed brown sugar
1 teaspoon vanilla
2 eggs
1 (12 ounce) package chocolate chips

Preheat oven to 375 degrees. Combine flour, baking soda, and salt. Cream shortening, sugars, vanilla, and eggs until fluffy. Add dry ingredients and chocolate chips to sugar mixture. Drop by teaspoonfuls onto ungreased cookie sheets. Bake 10 minutes.

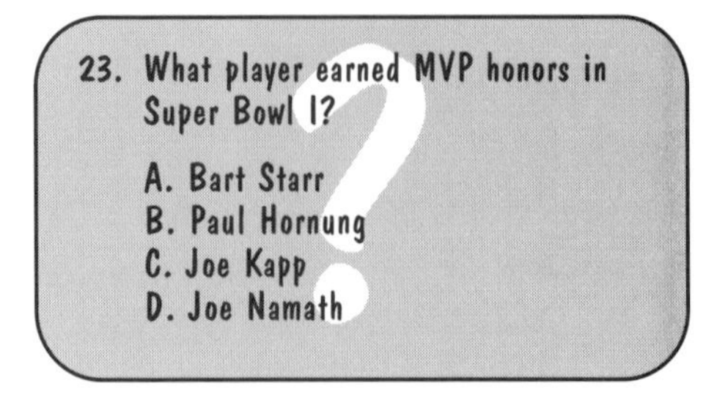

23. What player earned MVP honors in Super Bowl I?

A. Bart Starr
B. Paul Hornung
C. Joe Kapp
D. Joe Namath

# Week 15

24. What team holds the record for the most consecutive home game wins?

# Menu #15

**Creamy Bacon Chip Dip**
**Hawaiian Style BBQ Ribs**
**Sensational Pecan Brownies**

## Creamy Bacon Chip Dip

1 tablespoon mayonnaise
2 teaspoons minced onions
2 teaspoons bacon bits
1 tablespoon Worcestershire sauce
1 (8 ounce) package cream cheese

Combine all ingredients and chill. Serve with your favorite potato chips.

## Hawaiian Style BBQ Ribs

3 racks ribs
1 tablespoon dark brown sugar, packed firmly
½ clove garlic
⅓ cup teriyaki sauce
⅓ cup ketchup

⅓ cup pineapple juice
1 tablespoon hot sauce

In a large Dutch oven cover ribs with water and bring to a boil for 5 minutes. Cover and remove from heat for 35 minutes. In a saucepan combine remaining ingredients and bring to a boil. Reduce heat and simmer for 12 minutes. Remove from heat and let cool. Preheat grill to medium and place ribs on grill. Grill ribs, covered, on each side 12 minutes per side. Brush ribs with sauce and cook for another 7 minutes per side.

## Sensational Pecan Brownies

1 box brownie mix
1 (4 ounce) box chocolate pudding mix, prepared
1 (12 ounce) container whipped topping
1 brownie mix with pecans

Bake brownies according to directions on box in a 9 x 13 pan and cool. Prepare pudding according to directions on the box. Let stand for 5 minutes then spread over brownies. Then cover pudding with whipped topping. Chill 4 hours before serving.

## PLAYER PROFILE

**Bob Lilly** was drafted to the NFL in 1961 from Texas Christian University. He was voted all-pro 7 times and played in 11 Pro Bowl games. When Lilly was elected to the Hall of Fame in 1980, it was a first for the Dallas Cowboys. Bob was born in Texas, went to college in Texas, and became a Hall-of-Fame football player in Texas. But that has not been the only place where Lilly has had an influence. Now a photographic artist, Lilly had a photo gallery in New Mexico from 1986-1989 and is involved in investments, digital computer imaging and retouching of photographs.

# Week 16

25. What team has scored the most points in a season?

# Menu #16

Taco Dip

Hawaiian Wings

Everybody's Favorite Cherry Cheesecake

## Taco Dip

1 large can refried beans
1 package taco seasoning
8 ounces prepared avocado dip
8 ounces sour cream
1 head lettuce, shredded
12 ounces shredded Cheddar cheese
2 tomatoes, diced
1 small can sliced black olives
1 Spanish onion, chopped

Blend refried beans and taco seasoning with mixer until smooth. Spread on large serving plate. Cover with avocado dip and then sour cream. Top with lettuce, cheese, tomatoes, olives, and onions. Serve with tortilla chips.

## Hawaiian Wings

3 pounds chicken wings
1 cup soy sauce
1 clove garlic, grated
½ cup brown sugar
2 tablespoons sesame seeds
3 chopped green onions

Wash and pat dry chicken. Mix soy sauce, garlic, brown sugar, sesame seeds, and green onions together and marinate chicken wings in this mixture overnight in the refrigerator (we use a plastic bag). Fry wings in 1 inch oil to light brown. Cool and dip in sauce and place on cookie sheet to reheat at 350 degrees to set the sauce.

## Everybody's Favorite Cherry Cheesecake

1 (16 ounce) package cream cheese
1 (14 ounce) can sweetened condensed milk
⅓ cup lemon juice
1 teaspoon vanilla extract
1 (9 inch) graham cracker crust
1 (21 ounce) can cherry pie filling

In a large bowl beat cream cheese until smooth. Gradually mix in the milk until smooth. Stir in lemon juice and vanilla. Pour into crust and chill for 4 hours. Top with cherries and enjoy.

# Week 17

26. What team has scored the most touchdowns in a single season?

# Menu #17

## Cheddar Potato Skins
## Chicken Rollups
## Texas Cookies

### Cheddar Potato Skins

Number of potatoes you wish to use
Shredded Cheddar cheese
Bacon bits

Pierce potatoes and bake in microwave oven till done, about 2 to 4 minutes each. Let cool. Slice in half lengthwise and scoop out potato, leaving the skin intact. Sprinkle skins with cheese and bacon bits. Broil until cheese melts or microwave on high for 1 ½ minutes for each potato.

### Chicken Crescent Rollups

2 cups diced chicken
½ cup shredded cheese
2 cans crescent rolls
1 can cream of chicken soup
1 cup milk

Preheat oven to 375 degrees. Combine chicken and cheese. Place spoonful of chicken mixture on each section of crescent roll and roll up as for crescent roll. Mix soup and milk. Place rolls in baking pan and pour soup mixture over top. Bake for 25 minutes.

## Texas Cookies

1 cup shortening
1 cup brown sugar
1 cup sugar
2 eggs
1 (12 ounce) bag chocolate chips
2 cups flour
2 cups quick oats
1 teaspoon baking powder

Preheat oven to 350 degrees. Mix together shortening, sugars, and eggs until smooth. Add remaining ingredients and mix well. Drop by teaspoonfuls on greased cookie sheet. Bake for 13 minutes.

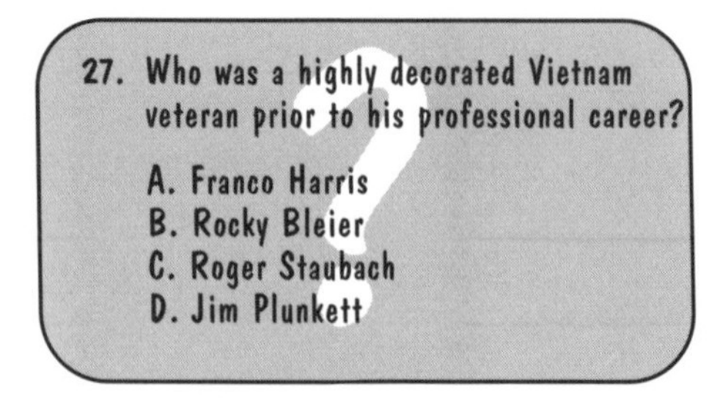

## PLAYER PROFILE

**Tony Dorsett**, 1976 Heisman Trophy winner and member of the College Football Hall Of Fame, was rookie of the year in 1977, a member of the Dallas Cowboys' Ring of Fame, and a member of the Pro Football Hall Of Fame. He was one of the most prolific running backs in the NFL. In addition to his athletic triumphs, Tony has accomplished a great deal off the field. He is involved in Players Inc., an investor in stocks and other businesses, a venture with his own athletic shoe company, and a great place called the Smoothies Factory. At the Smoothies Factory they serve drinks made from fresh fruits, ice, and nutritious supplements.

# Superbowl Sunday Spectacular

28. Who has thrown the most touchdown passes in his career in the Super Bowl?

# Superbowl Menu

**Steve's Super Stuffed Mushrooms**

**Super Bowl-You-Over Chicken Chili**

**Goal Post Steak Kabobs**

**Ed's MVP Ice Cream Pie**

## Steve's Super Stuffed Mushrooms

24 large mushrooms
¼ cup chopped onions
Pinch of garlic salt
¼ cup butter
⅔ cup dry bread crumbs
½ cup shredded cheese [of your choice]

Wash and drain mushrooms. Remove stems and save caps off to the side. Chop up stems, to make one cup. In a saucepan cook stems, onion, and garlic salt in butter until tender. Stir in bread crumbs and cheese. Spoon mixture into mushroom caps. Place in a 15 x 10 inch baking dish. Bake at 425 degrees for 10 minutes.

## Super Bowl-You-Over Chicken Chili

1 chicken, boiled, skinned and deboned
3 cans white beans (Great Northern or Navy)
1 tablespoon vegetable oil
1 medium chopped onion
3 garlic gloves, minced
5 tomatillos, husk and stem end removed, finely chopped
1 (16 ounce) package frozen white corn
1 tablespoon cumin
2 tablespoon chili powder
1 tablespoon crushed red pepper
1 teaspoon cayenne pepper
1 teaspoon oregano
2 (4 ounce) cans green chiles
2 cups chicken broth
2 tablespoon lemon juice
1 tablespoon dried cilantro

Boil the chicken in enough water to cover for 1 hour. Save broth. Place the white beans in a large pot. Set over low heat. Heat the oil in a skillet over medium heat and saute the onion and garlic until golden. Debone the chicken and add to beans. Stir the sauteed ingredients into the bean and chicken mixture, along with all remaining ingredients except lime juice and cilantro. Simmer uncovered 1–2 hours. Just before serving, stir in lime juice and cilantro.

## Goal Post Steak Kabobs

¼ cup butter, melted
¼ cup cilantro, chopped
¼ teaspoon garlic seasoning
½ teaspoon hot sauce
2 ears of corn, husked and halved
8 red cherry peppers
1 pound sirloin steak, cut into one inch cubes

Combine butter, cilantro, garlic seasoning, and hot sauce in a bowl. Heat grill. Alternately place corn, peppers, and steak onto four skewers. Place skewers on grill at medium heat. Brush on butter mixture often while cooking till meat is done to desired taste.

**29. What team holds the record for the most consecutive home losses?**

**A. Buccaneers**
**B. Chargers**
**C. Cowboys**
**D. Lions**

## Ed's MVP Ice Cream Pie

1 (9 inch) graham cracker pie crust
1 quart vanilla ice cream
½ cup chocolate syrup
1 container whipped topping

Soften ice cream and spoon half into the pie crust. Place in freezer for 5 minutes. Remove from freezer and pour chocolate syrup over ice cream evenly. Spoon remainder of cream on top of the syrup. Freeze overnight and top with whipped topping before serving.

# Field Goal Menus

## (a few extras just in case you need the points)

### Three Point Bean Dip

1 can refried beans
1 (8 ounce) package cream cheese
1 (16 ounce) container sour cream
1 package taco mix

Mix all ingredients well and pour into baking dish. Bake at 350 degrees for 20 minutes. Serve with tortilla chips.

### Wide Right Taco Salad

1 pound hamburger
1 head lettuce, shredded
1 cup grated Cheddar cheese
1 onion, chopped
1 bag tortilla chips
1 (16 ounce) can kidney beans, drained
4 tomatoes, chopped
1 bottle taco sauce

Cook hamburger and drain. Mix all remaining ingredients in salad bowl and add hamburger. Top with taco sauce.

## Extra Point Coleslaw

1 head cabbage, chopped
1 ½ cup grated carrots
1 bunch celery, chopped
¼ cup mayonnaise

Combine all ingredients in a bowl and toss. Cover and chill in refrigerator overnight.

## Dog Pound Chow

1 package semi-sweet chocolate chips
1 stick margarine
1 cup peanut butter
1 box Crispix cereal
4 cups powdered sugar

Melt chocolate chips and margarine together. Add 1 cup of peanut butter. Pour over the Crispix cereal. Pour cereal into a paper bag with the powdered sugar. Shake till all is mixed well.

## Goal Line Stand Chicken Fajitas

2 tablespoons lime juice
1 tablespoon minced onion
1 garlic clove, minced
½ teaspoon salt, pepper
1 pound boneless, skinless chicken breast
1 package flour tortilla shells
2 cups lettuce, shredded
1 tomato, diced
1 jar salsa

Combine lime juice, onion, garlic, salt, and pepper in a shallow dish. Add chicken and coat well. Cover dish and refrigerate overnight. The next day grill chicken breast for 5 minutes per side. Cut into ¼-inch strips. Place on tortillas and top with lettuce, tomato, and salsa.

## In The Trenches Fried Chicken

1 cup crushed corn flakes
½ teaspoon poultry seasoning
¼ teaspoon pepper seasoning
¼ cup plain yogurt
4 boneless, skinless chicken breasts

Combine flakes and seasonings in a shallow pan. Dip chicken lightly with yogurt. Roll in flake mixture. Place in baking pan and cook at 400 degrees for 45 minutes.

## Halftime Pizza Omelet

4 tablespoons chopped onion
½ pound ground beef
½ cup sliced mushrooms
4 tablespoons chopped tomato
4 tablespoons chopped green pepper
½ teaspoon garlic powder
½ teaspoon oregano
5 eggs
1 cup shredded Cheddar cheese

Saute onion. Add ground beef, cook and drain. Add the remaining vegetables and spices. Simmer for 2 minutes. Beat together the eggs and cheese and add 2 tablespoons of water. Place beef and vegetables into a greased baking dish. Pour the egg mixture over top and bake at 450 degrees for 20 minutes.

## Overtime Cake

1 German chocolate cake mix, prepared
1 jar caramel topping
1 jar fudge topping
1 (12 ounce) container whipped topping
1 cup chopped nuts

Bake cake according to box mix directions. Warm caramel and fudge toppings. Pour toppings over the cake. Place in the refrigerator until cool. Serve with whipped topping and nuts.

## Red Zone Cheesecake

1 (9 inch) graham cracker pie crust
24 ounces whipped topping
24 ounces cream cheese
2 cups sour cream
1 jar strawberry sauce

Mix whipped topping, cream cheese, and sour cream together and pour into pie crust. Top with strawberry sauce and chill in refrigerator before serving.

## Time-Out Chow Mein Noodle Cookies

1 (12 ounce) package butterscotch chips
1 (12 ounce) package chocolate chips
2 cans chow mein noodles

Melt chips together. Remove from heat and stir in noodles. Drop by teaspoon onto wax paper and let set till firm.

30. What player holds the record for the longest rushing touchdown?

A. Tony Dorsett
B. Billy Sims
C. Marcus Allen
D. Emmit Smith

# Answers to Trivia Questions

1. George Seifert
2. B
3. Pittsburgh at Denver
4. C
5. Detroit lost to Denver
6. George Blanda
7. Lenny Moore
8. D
9. Morten Anderson
10. Barry Sanders
11. B
12. D
13. Dan Marino
14. B
15. Phil Sims
16. Carolina and Dallas
17. D
18. Dallas
19. San Francisco vs. Denver
20. 104 yards by Jack Tatum
21. B
22. United States Naval Academy
23. A
24. Miami
25. Washington
26. Miami
27. B
28. Joe Montana
29. C
30. A

# List of Recipes

## First Half Appetizers



## The Half Time Show

## The Last Half (How Sweet It Is!)



## Field Goal Menus
## (A few extras just in case you need the points)

# Acknowledgments

I would like to thank my family, Jerri, Jenny, and Cory, and my parents, Vivian and Ed Sr., for their love and support, especially during the football season. Also, a big thanks to my co-workers who supported me and listened to me talk about this project for the last year.

ED BARTKO

I would like to thank my wife, April, and my son, Phillip, for being patient with me during the writing of this book. Not only did it take time away from them, they had to try everything I cooked.

STEVE LONG

# About the Authors

**Ed Bartko** is a thirty-eight-year-old regular guy, who is married and has two children, a daughter twelve, and a son nine. Ed is native to northwest Ohio. Ed graduated from Cardinal Stritch High School and Owens Technical School. Ed is currently a dairy manager with a local grocery store chain. Ed enjoys his family, golf, football, baseball, and anything else that is somewhat round and is hit, kicked, or thrown. Ed is interested in making life better for the regular guy by sharing what he likes from the viewpoint of a regular guy. This usually includes food. Ed has given much thought to the contents of the *2 Regular Guys Cookbook*. Ed's contribution to the cookbook has been creativity, diversity of food, and making sure that there is nothing fat free in the book.

**Steve Long** is a thirty-eight-year-old regular guy, who is married and has one child, a son who is three years old. Steve was born in Texas but raised in northern Ohio. He graduated from the University of Central Florida, and Midwestern Baptist Theologic[al] Seminary in Kansas City, Missouri. Currently the pastor of a Baptist church in Oregon, Ohio, Steve enjoys his family and watching and playing sports. Watching sports gives him a chance to discover and try new food, and that makes sports watching all the better. He's sharing these recipes with regular guys to make their sports watching more enjoyable. The best part is that Steve gets to test everything first.

Ed and Steve are pictured on the cover.